Water from a toad

A Book of Poems

By
Frederick E. Whitehead

No Frills
<<<>>>
Buffalo

Copyright ©2012 by Frederick E. Whitehead

Printed in the United States of America
Whitehead, Frederick E.

Water From a Toad/ Whitehead 1st Edition

ISBN: 978-0615708003

Poetry

Cover art - The Toad - ©2012 by David Thiel

Linoleum Print - Toad ©2012 by Frederick E.
Whitehead

No Frills Buffalo
119 Dorchester Road
Buffalo, New York 14213

Visit Nofrillsbuffalo.com

Water from a toad

my ocean

industrial torment
has left her
not a hypnotizing
azure of, say,
the waters embracing the Bahamas

cold until mid July most years
no seamless stretches of beach

she's shallow, stormy, sullen
she drinks in the Detroit
and pisses out the Niagara
under the bridge of peace

now with lateen full,
a steady breeze
propels my small craft
across her uncommonly
smooth skin

I turn into the sun
that goes to rest
at her far end,
steady the sail
and listen for
her ancient wisdom

sweet spaces

I knew there would be
sweet spaces in his senility
moments
filled with phrases
only the enlightened
of the world
would understand

I would shift restlessly
waiting for those times

learning the art of
code breaking
I would sit between the
machinery and bedrail
watching for the telltale
brightening of his eyes
anticipating the brief
straightening of the spine
that would signify the coming
of some great insight
he may have been
meditating on for years

one, only now
allowed to slip
through loose threads

in the faded tapestry
of his life

then this giant of a man
would again be in conversation
with any
number of people
but me
the only other
person in the room

vulturus

lacking the proper
apparatus for vocalizing
his joy
as do the gulls
in the city,
he grunted
a small prayer of thanks
and silently
went to work on
the glorious feast
laid out before him
near mile marker 218

anxious ivory beak,
efficient in design,
moved through
the main course
without much pageantry
no company
save an armadillo
lollygagging
amongst
the scrub

book

there are bones to be excavated
deep within these ancient pages
under dust of allegory and supposition

a sapphire framework
to which all things mythical
cling so desperately to
one hand gripping as tight as it can
the other waiving for attention

residual heart effect

the streets we
used to run
have been
widened now
just enough to
allow for sidewalks

recent additions
not in the
photos I came across today

there was one of her
standing with arms raised
where the lawn met the street
the ground wet from
the spray of a hose
a bike on its side
a sweatshirt abandoned by
one of the trees that
used to tower above us

thinking it was dusty
I swiped my thumb
across the photo
a kid took on
some spring afternoon

when plans were big
and everything was possible

it wasn't dusty at all
just faded

under

under
canvas awning rain
Spanish café
in a small ocean-side village
a colorful drink centered
on a cork circle at my elbow
a platter of shrimp
a cigar

there
as the storm spirits
rise from baked stone walkways
I could
try to find
a different way to
encounter
my own personal reality

never again will I
view the world from under
hood of slow execution

my eyes will take in
reflected light
invert and split the invisible
bands into color and
ready the information
for processing

but that's all they will do

my eyes
were not employed for seeing,
that particular duty
belongs to the
heart

one that has been blind
for too long
set blind
by frustrated busyness
faulty temperament
unacknowledged language

there, winding my tongue
around new dialect
I could speak myself
into a world I knew of
only through tales
of old men

there, to let
the saline wind
blow across my
low slung shoulders
taking with it what of
me it can carry

water from a toad

having no aboriginal
shaman to turn to
I have to search for answers in the
general noise and
confusion that surrounds me

am I really more intelligent
than the common mouse?
probably not
would Darla choose me over Alfalfa?
why is ear wax only available
in one color?

this is why I
I really need to pal around with
a jovial guy in a loincloth
he alone could help me
make sense of the universe
or in the very least, make me
feel a little more normal
in an un-normal world
we could be there
teacher and student
on a street corner
in the oppressive
heat of the city,

me with my cola
him squeezing water
from a toad

autumn

came
to me,
by the woodpile
with the split
and stacked cherry
the oak
the ash
the splitter quiet
ticking down to cool again,
it was there,
a voice first came

I leaned against the shed
listening, absently watching
the empty cornstalks
move solemnly through
their stationary final waltz,
trying to decipher words
that only hinted at clarity

a gentle force come to
steer me from
that of which
I should be
steered from

toward a door
thought to be
so unapproachable

for all those years
when I gathered up
breakable things
all around me, counting
their worth by their numbers alone
and packing days with
hours stitched together so
tightly that I could
no longer fit myself in

I'm not on the threshold yet
but I can see
the door, so
sure that I'll
answer it
when I knock

by the lake, walking

the waves o'er the break wall surge
the lake wind stabs into my lungs
I walk with song that seem to urge
me sing, lest it's never sung

along the plankwalk above the sand
above the rocks and dead drift piled
the shifting line where lake meets land
a foamy serpent stretched a mile

and I walked there most alone
a few birds maybe, on the pier
I longed to make my song be known
but not a soul to hear was there

dusklight then began to birth
tendrils of crimson, tangerine
from the vast horizons curve
yet die they did, stars were seen

stars which I let guide me home
stars to which I've closed my eyes
stars I wished had never shone
stars that whispered to my cries

travelers

lumbering forward
toward transcendence
each with their carapace
balanced, a hard

slow slag, the context
categorized of their days
(inglorious sameness)
the previous a twin of the next

Lech-Lecha, unswayed
each one went
forward always forward bent
having been told the way

earth breathing

it takes time
to learn
to be
the breath
that slow rise
in the morning
that soft decent
of returning
evening
earth breathing

candle, I

I
light the
candle the
vapor the bright
luminescence the
vanishing wax
which part of
this am
I

Sonny

I believe I will,
now that mine
has been nearly forgotten
around here anyway,
change my name

I think I will take the one
abandoned in death
by the southern born
owner of the filling station
that stood on one of the last
undeveloped sections of my town

I could pull off the ruse
by wearing a beat up Sinclair Oil hat
and by greeting folks in that slow
friendly conversation that eases
a person into the day

I would continue his tradition
of handing out STP and Thrush
stickers to the neighborhood boys
and get a machine like
the one he used to have,
the kind that dispensed
cola in 10 oz. bottles for a quarter

and after I replaced the missing church key
that used to hang on a chain
nailed into the frame of
the garage window
I would open a bottle
sit on stacked crates of oil
just outside the bay door
and slowly turn back the world

master of imagination

if the master of imagination
would, just once,
offer me a place on knee
and instruct me in the ways
of translating
small wondrous things
or give me a position,
tending to the upkeep of
the lodges
the one in the forest
or the one lakeside

there I could let the music
in those walls
find its way
into me
with every pass
of the dusting rag

in their gardens of word
I would tend selective
well into winter
when, logging the hearth
for guests
who arrive
empty vessels
and leave overflowing

I would gather the remains
of the season
and arrange them
on the shelves in my room

mail

juggling drive-through coffee
and plastic sacks of groceries
she tilted her head
toward the mail fanned out
on the driveway
after a fumbling,
wrong handed retrieval
from the box
a single pale yellow envelope
stood out
among plain white utility bills
ad flyers
bank statements
other crap
funny, how
she told herself,
that this yellow
rectangle was the letter,
sent by the boy
who lived at the corner,
lost some decades and
finding its way to her now,
she was sure she would
recognize his blocky script
after even this amount
of past had passed
she awkwardly stooped

and scooped the mail up
sighing away
the way it turned out
to be just an envelope
of a different color
another flicker
of history
triggered by memories
and edited
for maximum
melancholic response

it's the fog, son

unexpected morning fog -
early owl eye sun
rises along
the seam of summer
bells of fuscia, dew damp,
wait
for warmth,

the peace of me
that I briefly find
fades
as my mind
settles on separation

knees

I'm fond of the way my
knees stop aching
an hour or so after
getting up in the morning
(twenty minutes more
if it's cold or humid)

hobbled as I am
I still enjoy the walk downstairs
to the bookshelves
to take in a sentence or two
to start my day
holding a book
at that magic distance
halfway between my nose
and the coffee maker

robbing the mystery

I realize now
that I don't want to know
that stars are only burning
orbs of gas, I want back
their tiny bit
of mystery,
robbed from me
in the third grade

and truth be told, any
knowledge of my DNA
or how closely my
ancestral line is tied to
that of the great apes,
I wouldn't mind
disposing of either,
its information that's
done precious little in moving me
in anything that could be
considered forward progression

and for that matter
let me return to believing
that snow is somehow magical
animals have the gift of language
and that all smiles are exactly
what they are meant to be

furthermore I most certainly
don't require the inside scoop concerning
the physics behind gravities pull
I simply want to believe again,
when leaping from rock
to rock while crossing a stream
that yes, even
if only for a second or two,
I can
fly

reaching

if there is
a plan for it all
I have a wish

to go quietly -
a prince of anomalies
with no knowledge

of where crystals of my
life may have landed
if I have touched

with a hand gentle,
and words undamaging
I don't need to know

for the unknown
is all I've ever
reached for

dawn poem

speckle of red
lost against
canvas of
warning sky
cardinal
whistled dawn
his poem
reading
as a lament

the new guys' rules

the first order of business
for the new Pharaoh was to
reinstate all of the old gods
gods for this
gods for that
gods with wide shoulders,
narrow waists and heads
of familiar animals

it would just be a
whole lot easier explaining
famine, war,
disease, failed love
and all the rest of it
if the team had
a little more depth
you know, it's not my fault
he could say
you guys just didn't pray enough
to the one with the cat head

the last pharaoh, with his
elongated cranium and almond
shaped eyes, his lovely wife
and single god, was miles away now
encased in resin and linen

his nose hacked off of statuary
his cartouches chiseled away
obelisks with newly blank spaces
cast long pointed shadows
over the sands of the confused
sky watching populace,
as they traced
the path of
their former deity
who seemed to be keeping
an eye on them nonetheless

lifestone

waiting with
mindeye
inward for
that stone to
share secrets
yes
waiting for pass-
age-
pass
in
hand
while storm
internal
races up
one appendage
down
another
a force
against
synching psyche
still the stone
holds out
still/life/stone
breath/thought/dreamdoubt
time
and time
how ages pass

while stone:life stills
the shudderance
of one

on an evening like this

when the combination
of breeze and low sun
is just right

nothing is
bothersome
and it's quiet enough
to catch up on
thoughts that matter

when I think
how truly lucky a man
would be that,
regardless of the form
the knife takes -
whether a look
a word
an action
a wish
whatever the form,
how lucky
he would be
to have
an angel knock
it from his grip

if luck holds out

long enough
he will learn to not
take up the knife
in the first place

shown upon departure

when my harmonic vibration
finally settles out

when I am gathered in again
with the rest of the light

I imagine myself in a field
in a room no longer there

under a ghost of a thatched roof
with my bare feet on foreign ground

the faint images of my lives
moving from periphery to focus

opening before me
as lessons etched on pages of crystal

I can feel fall

I can feel fall
not in the air,
no, I feel it
in that crease on my
back, where from I'm told
wings once grew
and fall feels
as if a certain smile
has gone missing
after taking
a lifetime to arrive

self made man

ignoring backs
bent below you
how it was
you can never forget
in your mighty hands
the golden wheel of your
star schooner,
riding high on seas
of fraudulent glory
she,
scuttled by circumstance
of your making alone

made to live low now
among those in whose
breast beat a collective
heart of servile insurrection
you wait now,
a dweller of trenches
wait, knowing
nothing is so
addictive than revenge
wait
for that first
lunge that will
bring them pleasure

no escape from these thoughts,
formulated in tar pit existence,
your blind stance
bound tragic
realities as if
with the very
shreds of her mainsail

let it be known
your prow tore through many
on the heading you took
you paid no heed
you proclaimed to have
had ownership of the wind
you felt yourself to
be the one thing that
one can never be
- a self made man

as a child

as a child I was told
to not play with matches
that guns are always loaded
and if I ran with anything
sharper than a balloon
I would most assuredly
fall, driving it cleanly
through my spleen
and I would be dead before my
mother could clean her hands
on her apron and come to see
what all the ruckus is about

I was also advised not to pick
a cat up by it's tail
snakes don't enjoy life in
a dresser drawer
and God apparently doesn't like
you much if you don't bathe regularly

also, my body, I was instructed,
was specifically
designed to block a line drive
grounder, dog crap doesn't pick itself
up and girls will hit back, usually
with good reason and pretty much
a lot harder

the fact was driven home
that if I stole even so much as
a gumdrop I would rot in San Quentin
"the place where Johnny Cash sings?"
I would ask
"he got beat up by bank robbers, so
he don't go there no more, but if
you steal anything I'll drive you there myself!"
I was told

I, of course, challenged all of
these guidelines,
save one
I'm still a pussy
when it comes to running
with anything pointy,
must be from my ignorance
of what a spleen is for
I would just prefer it
stays intact anyway

recounting my suicide for the soul committee

naked
I stood on the scale
and looked down past my
belly and pecker as the pointer
found center on
one hundred and twenty eight

I thought of how the scene would
look from the vantage point
of the vestibule, opted for
clothing, got dressed and reweighed
myself
one hundred thirty
I calculated my weight
against the drop
and envisioned clichéd images
of relatives waiting on
golden streets in
softly hued landscapes

I measured out the
proper length of line

thirteen knots would have been
symbolic of some satanic connection
to guilt, so I went with fourteen,

secured the line to the railing,
(close to an upright for
added strength)
and adjusted the business end
for just the right fit
just above Adams apple,
along chin line,
behind ears,
cinched up with
the first twist nicely tucked
under the knob on
the back of my skull

I coiled the rope
near my left foot
and stood with my hands
in my pockets
I thought how good I looked
in the jeans and shirt
I had chosen for the trip
aimed for the peacock
motif mosaic'd in the floor below
and took that
so often referenced
first step

ugly

with any amount of
reckoning it's evident that

we've little else but
a tenuous grasp

on sanity, a minor
infraction comes along

and any one of us
is more than capable

of a momentary display
of frightful madness

momentary is allowed
in fact, practically required

it's when it becomes a lifestyle
that things get ugly

collage

it is a distance
measured in
the unwelcomed
deflection of peace

that inevitable terrifying
abandonment of memory
that critical measurement
of distance
from the form
and the substance of
ones being
calculated from a moment lost
then another
then another

until only sparks
of a life
come in
as comets
low and fast
turning in time
to ashes
and floating into
their proper places
a collage for
others to decipher

it was a newt I think

I can't be certain
but I recall them from
when I was a kid and
this one had the
same orange spots

and this lizard that I took
for a newt stopped
about halfway across the
porch rail, in the damp shadow
of the quart sized beer can
and said to me

"this world of ours,
and yes, I do mean ours,
is really nothing more than
the firing of a neurotransmitter
in the
mind of some being
no language can describe"

and as if that wasn't weird enough,
he then stayed for an uncomfortably
long period of time
his small blue tongue
just barely visible in
what appeared to

be a grin
and waited for a response

a long period of time

finally gathering myself
I said
"sure, o.k."

"well" said newt "just thought you
should know, I'm off"
"my friend" I said as I leaned back
and pulled my cap over my eyes
"everybody's a little off"
and welcomed the sweet reality
of an honest afternoon nap

Platosphere

listening to
Crepuscule with Nellie
laying on the couch
and wondering how

the cat managed to
get the feather duster
out from behind the oversized
head of Plato staring
ever upward from his station
on the fireplace mantle

seeing the vanquished bird
in the middle of the floor
I thought
to retrieve it

it can wait
two minutes and
a half I said to the Greek

he didn't argue
so I closed my eyes
listened and wondered
if he ever
pounded out philosophy

while wearing
a cool looking hat

so, you're a poet now?

after a long pull from his beer
he wiped the cloud of foam
from his lip

then he asked me
so, you're a poet now?

me, being one
with a natural tendency
to, whenever possible,
elevate myself above
my pedestrian caste
answered
yea, I reckon I am

the fact that
I had yet to
earn the right to poetry
played little part in my answer

I do like the label however,
although it holds nothing of the importance
of husband
father
friend
it sure sounds pretty good

it has a casual way of
sitting in the crook of a
conversation
that word poet

nestled in the branches
of daily discourse
barely noticed until
the wind dies down
and troubles settle out

then poet, however briefly,
is looked upon
and wondered about

augmenting my illusion

mucking out the
chicken coop
stooped under its low roof
proof that
even within
these limits of
the city
I can be of the earth

trimming limbs
from the pear tree
the apple tree
in This small yard
fifteen by forty
cutting back old
for new

you letting me
be as much as
a farmer as is allowed
by circumstance

you know I would house
a goat in the garage
if I could get away with it
I haven't tried to put
that over yet

so I'll dig the tubers
pick the berries
and hide in the three small
rows of corn when I can

pretending
when you call from
the window
that your voice is traveling
across acres

to augment
my illusion
I'll walk
back to the house
as slow as I can
making tractor noises
under my breath
in my head
a hearty call
to hogs that are
not there

under scars

in her twenties
she was cut four times
a scalpel hewn
doorway for
my brothers and I
that we may leave
our first home
screaming in the
light our lungs
expanding with the cast off
breath of those who
were there before we
were there we
wiped clean
laid on her breast to
beat our hearts in syncopated
meter with hers
a few days shy of seventy
she was opened again
her insides
having rebelled
then surrendered
another scar another mark
in her travelogue
under those scars
is the place I began
away in ever widening

circles I move
picking up
things she left for me
which I return to her
on my visits as if
I was the first ever
to have discovered them
she smiles
a servant now
to her solitude
silent mostly but
seemingly assured
that she was as good
a guide as there could
have been her hair now
grown back enough so that I
have to brush it from
her forehead a kiss there
her eyes letting me know
it is not complete
I have got
so much more to do

spider monkey

uncountable
the stones removed
for your creation

a celestial collective waited
to witness your rise from Nazca
waited for prophecy to thaw

convey yourself
out of
the common mass
of your aboriginal brethren
beside you on the plain

the tarantula always
anticipating prey
that never shows itself
the thunderbird who
never takes rise
on Andean winds

go, as you've always wished
smell the Ceylon blooms
of Kira Khatun
shun the provincial shine

think strange

find and lose not the sight of
the precept golden
as your frame travels
among the unknowing

the years found you
your tail forever curled
your eyes only seeing sky
you longed for the
ill fitting flesh
of creatures nomadic

now, as you wander
let the empty space
within your form be filled
with the chants of Tibet
the waters of the Nile
the sun of the east

recite your life
to all things sentient
recite your life
to all things not
recite as red dust falls
from your twelve digits

rise to follow the
song of the spotted eagle
echo it with your

empty lungs
leave the familial
lament of the stationary
move

a sigh deeper

a sigh
deeper
a straightening of phrase
behind a wall of crepe
and petal

a hand goes
to cheek
before thoughts of
obligation
forehead after

leaning
on specifics
exhausted

the door at the edge of
the world
has never
been locked

still
it
has yet
to be tried

two

dusk creeps
round shouldered
over the hills
dampening the valley
with it's slow cold breath
as the man with
rucksack (canvas and strapped)
heads for the cabin

inside the lamps trimmed
burning, cook stove warm
inside, he puts the pack by
the door
inside he kisses the forehead
of the woman
who never learned
how to stop being beautiful

he'd been gone three days
he'll stay five
before leaving again
his bag of tools on his back
piecework in town for
the few dollars they need
but now he's here

they eat
they talk they laugh
she reads him the letter
from her sister in Kentucky
long now a widow, who met
a merchant man who asked her
to move north to Cincinnati
to wed

it may do her good, he says,
she never got on well alone
near as I can tell
we have enough saved you can
take the train to
see her get hitched
if you want
maybe, she says, and puts the letter
on the sideboard

the lamps out
both of them knowing that
she won't go
having not been more than
two miles apart from one another
for fifty three years
as dusk moved on and dark moved in
they slept
together apart
from the world beyond their valley

observation: winter midnight away from city dissonance

the silence of it
harboring its own extrapolation of pi
each moment floats off,
stellar spirits come to
inhabit briefly a time
linear, measured by intrinsic
early extinguished sun
nocturnal escape
christen it ethereal
entering this, have i
order? secure perhaps
for this serene,
insular winter sigh
the silence of it

sing

night hounds drag
corpses of conscience
past fire raged windows
nailed against
feral streets
delirium tremens
in one bulb rooms
wanting to dredge up pain
in order to sing
just
to
sing

eulogy

whatever beach
you find yourself on
waiting for the fishes
to stick their heads

out of the water
to turn their
attention shoreward

the beach
in that moment
will be yours alone

surely, they will listen
yours, a life spent
getting the eulogy just right
practiced on birds

ran by reptiles
even mammals not unlike
yourself, all blinking
without much
interest

the fish, they
who hold history of

every human
utterance thus far

they, whose chronicles
are kept orderly
for others who
number less
than stars
seen at dawns breaking
they must care
it is, after all,
worded so beautifully

cup, runneth etc.

twice now
two times in four days
I got the cup down
set it on the cutting board
and poured coffee onto it

I say onto it
because it was, as were
my thoughts, upside down

I've been finding
myself making
repeated trips
up and down stairs
for something left
up when I needed it down
down when I wanted it up

Lately
I rarely know what day it is
until I've been in it for a while
I don't even care anymore
what is a day anyway
little things slip out
of the grey
making way
for other little things

all pouring into me
until the day
I turn over
and it all spills off my back

there was a time

there was a time when
the search for peaceful
cohabitation was
foremost in my usage of time
a doe eyed expedition
through the darkened
landscape of confused opposites
I, by luck or providence,
found it
and wear it as
comfortably as
a favorite sweatshirt

now it would seem
that small conversations
on the happenings
of our days and a chair
with proper
lumbar support
is about all I need
in the bliss department

that and at least two
uninterrupted hours
in middle afternoon
with nothing to do

yes, that and a cat
willing to trade
an air of faithfulness
for a spot in my lap as
the nights creep toward
sub freezing

and let's not forget
a book, one with
ideas wholly unoriginal
but worded so brilliantly
that a spark of insight
flashes momentarily
beneath my graying scalp
just before sleep
wins again

house arrest

another afternoon
meditating on criminal
depravity
with a bowl of pretzels

I crunch on
arson rape murder
I chew on images of
embezzlement
kidnappings
terror in American homes
all this
and
more until the
bowl is empty

I push around the salt
at the bottom
with a dampened finger
stretching my interpretation
of horror

a spiral downward
only halted
by a granddaughter bursting
into the room
with flowers pilfered

from the neighbors garden
this too a crime

a crime
of innocence true enough
but as I watch another
war raging on the
television beyond
her gap-toothed smile
I can't help but think

maybe
if only for her own good
a couple years of
house arrest
just might
be in order

the lasting effects of late night television
circa 1972

the twigs stacked
by the fence
appeared in the long
shadows of the morning
like giant arachnids

those who didn't
make it through - such as
ones cut down
en masse
in battle
in some glorious end
to a grainy science fiction film
of my boyhood

the dew steaming off
the entangled limbs
as the sun found its way
to them from
behind the peak of
the garage
added to the effect

so much so
that I found myself
closing the kitchen window

turning the latch slowly
into place
and squinting at the pile
over my raised coffee mug

readying myself
for flight
at even the slightest
evidence of a sequel

another thing fishing does

8 ft. bamboo pole
12 or so feet of line
a cork a hook a worm
and all afternoon
to think of little things

like the old guy
that lived next door to us
he died on the table
undergoing a routine procedure

did I say anything
to him that morning as
he left his house alone?
I'm sure he
waved cheerfully
"good morning there"
he may have said
"hi" I could have answered

the cork sinks below
the surface
a short tug
it comes back up and stays

as he backed his Buick
out, past the hedge where I was

trying to find the baseball that
got by me
did he look to see if I was waving
goodbye?
I might have
I don't recall now

I set the pole down in the grass
pull a beer from the cooler
and raise a toast to the sky
forty years too late

trash

the city designated
weekend for purging
(circled in red since
February) finally arrived

a warm afternoon
found me dragging
overstuffed boxes
loosely tied bundles
armload after armload
to curbside

when done
another beer cap twisted
I sit on the tailgate of my
truck and wait for
the scrappies to show up

their bald-tired wrecks
low and angry
some prowling by slow
a weathered face squinting
out of the passenger side window
others would side up
to the curb, practically
ejecting someone to
snatch a bit of metal and

move off quickly to a pile
further up the street

like a dingo ripping off a
chunk of meat and
running ahead of
the pack

some would politely ask if they
could have my orphaned bits
of life - to which I would
answer - sure I'm done
with 'em - but only
if their attire suited
their intentions
tattered flannel shirts
oily jeans leather work gloves
an honest mans wardrobe

I would deny such gifts
to the clean ones
sauntering out of new trucks
their designer shades
crisp shirts neat hair
it's them
I don't trust
there is something
disingenuous in their manner

I won't have the
likes of them
rifling through my
perfectly proportioned
pile of discarded memorabilia

them I send away
with a smattering of
profanities and a thumb
hooked in the
direction of elsewhere

a dessert - personal (of course)

a day made for manna
directionless, hunger setting in, on
any other day, I'd've not known
yearning, but this, this... a
morning darkmarked it would seem
a morning created specifically for
doing anything possible to
earn any favor the sky may offer, if
failing hours up the ante
or I am left, still stranded
remembering how easy life has been, a
memory risen as a lesson, a ram,
a pardon, a way
never doubt deliverance, this, a
new promise to be had
a day made for manna

tierce

the pen
is most lazy tonight
lounging
with its cap pulled
down tight
next to
the journal
who tries to motivate
it with suggestions
of story lines
that revolve around sticky
social situations

what about insightful
observations on the
curiosities of the day?
the journal asks

the antics of animal life?
colorfully elaborated tales
of youthful adventure?

seriously? no commentary on
treachery and unrest
from misunderstood corners
of the world ?

the pen snorts but
doesn't budge

the lamp
watching
from the corner of the desk
weighs in on this exchange
by retiring its light
the pen yawns
the journal stops trying
the lamp nods

and with little fanfare
the final notes
of King Solomon's Marbles
guides the trio into
unconsciousness

one more thing

since you have asked

I may have forgotten
to mention
a particular part
of the story

About
how I would take up
a cup of coffee
and walk the planked
walk down to
and beyond the dune line

this, before the sun graced
the horizon
this, below fading constellations
this, as mother turtles
returned to the surf

without looking back
at the mounds
of sand that marked
the places where they
had labored

did I touch upon
how the feeding
birds seemed to be
in a contra dance
with the waves?
this comparison
came to me as I walked
my feet following
no set path
among the deposited shells

did we talk at all about
the way the air
felt lighter there?
if not, my apologies,
but the air most
certainly felt
lighter there

and, if I failed to mention
how the ocean sounded
like a choir
you will have to forgive
me, my mind
tends to veer off
on occasion
my thoughts helplessly
tossed about

with other debris
gathered on that shore

anyway, the turtles
the mounds
and as I've said,
the beach

and eventually the sun
did arrive

breaking the plane
of dawn
illuminating me
as I tried to
forget the city

preservation

my
diet
it derived
from beds raised and timbered
souled with soil
of my own making

truest old seed
honest tuber
trees shouldering fruit
I accept, as from
vine and bush and grass

offerings
taken
when from
our star again,
this modest plot
of earth tilts

the angels got involved

again
I can picture them rolling
their eyes
getting up from the couch
or putting down the rake
they will shrug and
clap the dust from
their hands
to pull me back from
the brink
again

they will tire of
this constant
deflection of danger
or stupidity eventually
letting me possibly
to set up a ladder clumsily
close to the power supply line
or allowing an icicle to fall
with deadly precision

if I follow the rules
close enough
they just might
let me fall asleep
in a hammock

my final dream
being
one of family or
a childhood pet
or maybe

one of an endless beach
the ocean breeze
carrying to me
the voice of my grandmother
saying how nice
it will be
to pick up the conversation
where we left off

Feng Shui my ass

my shin
is the last to learn of
the new configuration
for the coffee table

having traversed these spaces
for years without incident
I've never noticed
anything amiss
concerning the energy here

but now,
as I massage
the divot in my leg,
while
the Siamese nuzzles
up against the table
right at the point
of the assault
(thereby letting me know
that it remains her property
regardless of placement),

I can't help but notice
an unmistakable
lowering in

the harmonic vibration
of the room

watchkeepers

tick off frostcoat
mornings inlaid
with firestoned eyes
shake woolened hands
stomp downed boot break
fast with the matriarchal
denizens
of dawning corners
air greased coffee drowned
conversation slow
around subjects half
interesting but easy
the tab can be ran until
Thursday so again a cup
the bell rings
your exit up the blue banked
avenue to do your ten
and a half
bent over the fortunes
of unseen men
with minute-clocked precision
memory locked in fingertips
fading elsewhere
the day automatic piled with
cough arthritic blind
clone after cloned
parts for industrial partitioning
clinging to what little
there is left
for you to do
until the bell
rings your exit back

down that washed
up road past the diner
the evening has waited
your return with
without prejudice
into woodstove
will go split palletwood
useless mail
the evening paper
unread
the news is never
worthy your attention
anyway

so special

so, in our audacity,
we claim the crown
of reflection
- claim dominion

all the time
trying to gather sense
of lights in the sky

often
with a shudder
the curtains are parted
and the wonder above
is scanned
age old speculation
balanced
against hope internal

if one of those
pinholes breaks loose
and happens by
in slow
observational
orbit

it can easily be imagined
that all
parties involved
will be
standing at their
windows
mouths agape

in unwilling acknowledgement
that the word special
doesn't really
apply anymore

a simple accidental moment

it was the kind of thing
that, had I not stopped
and got in close,
something so small
yet so grand
would never
have been noticed
much less given
any thought

a simple accidental moment
offered
so I could
watch the monarch
shifting position
ever so slightly
in order to
partake of nectar
then
lifting away
when done

leaving flecks
of wingdust
nearly microscopic
where she had been
had I not slowed down
that one time
those colors would have
(as I'm sure so much in
life's spectrum has before)
been lost to me

a spouses glance
a child's laugh
a friends troubles
an apology
a bit of praise
small answers to
big questions, all gone

with little but
the smudged markings
of hectic choice
left behind

fox

as my breath rose to meet
the dawn crossing our paths
I saw her
by the gut pile,
red over red
no hunt required
she put away all she needed
and moved on

a place for giveness

this lane
insular
winding,
I find myself
from time to time, on it
- to an abandoned cabin
birch trees tower and shed
the pond receives visitors
the sloping terrain goes off
in all directions
in this pocket
I place myself
the creak of the rocking chair
accentuating the thoughts of all
of those to which I've
brought disharmony
pain of heart
corruption of conscience

I give my apologies unto
the slow uplifting breeze here
- that they may
make their way

I stay until
there is just
enough light
to find my way out
always hoping
I'll be able to
find my way in again

In the bestiary of my imagination

In the bestiary
of my imagination
there are common family
dilemmas among
the creatures there

who is to carry
the eggs back
to the tunnels
if you were
let's say, a middle ant
taking orders via pheromones
from those hatched
possibly
only days before you were

the Queen cares not to listen
to such grievances
just do as your brother,
he's done it before
and knows how it's
to be done

what of the jay
having spent every hour
for a week straight building
a perfectly suitable nest
in a spot
out of the elements
under the eve
of the woodshed
landing proudly

with what he had hoped
to be the last bit of dry grass
for the lining
only to lose the same argument
males have lost forever
on matters domicile

and one can't forget
the mallard
in her immodest garb
relegated by some outdated
tradition
to stay nearly silent
and always two
paces behind
her flamboyant mate
for life
and he
returning to the same
spot again this year
only, this time without her
walking towards the
edge of the pond
he looks back
every so often
before entering the water
perhaps wishing no longer
to float

Water from a toad

About the Author

Frederick E. Whitehead lives and works in
Buffalo NY.

Water From a Toad is his fourth collection of
poetry.

Other titles from the author are:
songs, cradled, *protected by paradox*, and *Orbs*.

www.ingramcontent.com/pod-product-compliance
Lightning Source LLC
Chambersburg PA
CBHW060819050426

42449CB00008B/1733